Americana

Americana

poems

TJ Beitelman

Black
Lawrence
Press

Black Lawrence Press
www.blacklawrence.com

Executive Editor: Diane Goettel
Book and cover design: Amy Freels

ISBN: 978-1-62557-919-5

Published 2015 by Black Lawrence Press.
Printed in the United States.

And one day we will die
and our ashes will fly
from the Aeroplane over the sea

But for now we are young
Let us lay in the sun
And count every beautiful thing we can see

—Neutral Milk Hotel

CONTENTS

1.
OCCASIONS

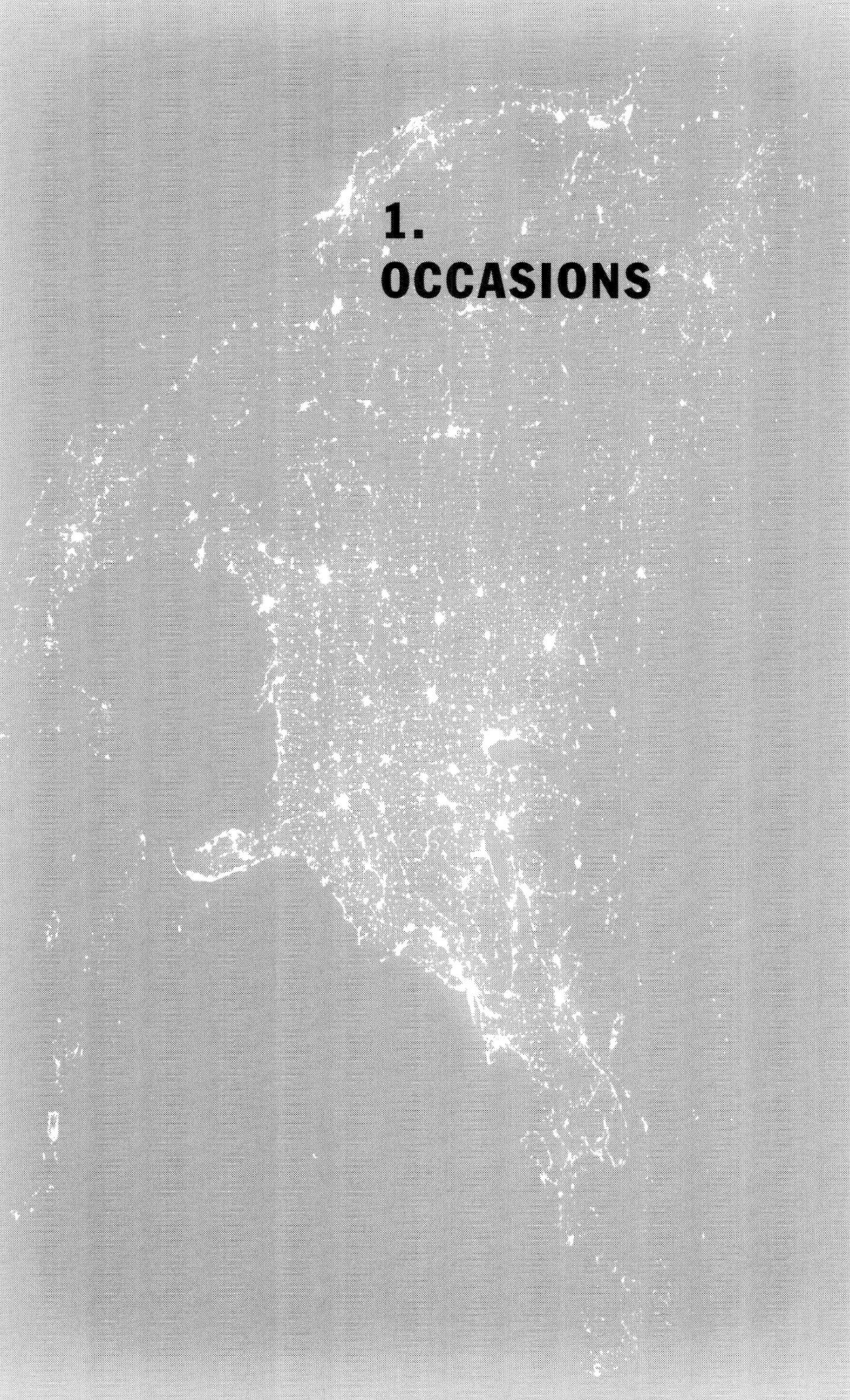

AN AUBADE FOR THE AFRICAN QUEEN AND ITS BIG BANG

Rose:	*I'm all turned around Charlie—which way is the east shore?*
Charlie:	*The way we're swimming old girl!*

Had I not been zooming through the Cosmos,
as yet unfettered by material forms, I could
have told Bogey: It's *always* the detonators
that take some doing. Everything's a powder
keg: a ratty vessel taking on water or a thimble-
sized universe. No matter—it's all waiting
to combust. The trick is the tinder. The spark.
The thing that transforms potential to kinetic.
Could be, yes, cartridges, nails, boxes of soft
wood—a makeshift torpedo at the water line.
But why think small? After all, *something*
touched off the exponential cosmic explosion
we're all swimming through. What're the odds
it was a broken boat, floating in wait? Billions
and billions to one. It had to be something
like a Rose: sharp-tongued, chiseled, gorgeous
with a dirty face, obvious in her catholic charms.
In the face of such a face, even Kaiser's doomed
navy men would freely choose to do the deed,
dutifully pledge to let no man put it asunder,
even as the impregnable world they know erupts.

UPON THE THIRTIETH ANNIVERSARY OF HANK AARON SURPASSING BABE RUTH AS ALL-TIME HOMERUN KING

The sky opened in the ten minutes it took to fete
Hank Aaron after he hit #715. Hank says time
paused as he was rounding the bases: the college
kids patting him on the back between second

and third might as well have been gnats or rain-
drops. . .O, the rain! Who was the first to think
the unthinkable?—*Wait, if this gets called, do we
go back to 714?* Tomorrow is another day, indeed.

Hank, the Buddhists say it is raining everywhere.
The greatest Zen masters proclaim their impotence:
*I cannot be a good Zen master; I have seen good Zen
masters.* As for me, I can't be a good homerun hitter—

that's no false modesty. Some things we just can't
do. But I've seen a lot of homeruns, Hank, and now
I suspect each one is nothing special, a single ball
socked into the night. Yes, they can be washed off

the books, even the momentous ones. Nothing
to do but wait and see if what we've seen is real.
We sit in our hard bleacher seats, hold the breath
we share. We stare straight up into the spitting sky.

A SONNET IN REMEMBRANCE OF BEING PROPOSITIONED DURING THE LAST INTERMISSION OF A TOM STOPPARD PLAY, BLACKSBURG, VIRGINIA, MARCH 18, 1995

By rights, I should've had a date that night,
with daisies in her hair. The kind of girl
who'd laugh at all the clever repartee:
when Rosencrantz tells Guildenstern that death

is just a boat, that every exit is
an entrance someplace else...That night, alas,
guffaws were few. Just mine to punctuate

the room. Curtain: *Enter* HARVEY, *right*.
He eyed me, smiled, and said, "You look neglected."
Dear Harvey, tell me this: Why are our hearts
so eager to connect? I'll hold my breath

for something witty. No—don't. My exodus—
(I stumbled off just as the house lights fell)
—confirms it: Blink and we evaporate.

UPON CHARLEY'S MARRIAGE TO A GIRL FROM IDAHO

My friend Charley cleans up real
nice and is handsome in his red
silk shirt. We are on the beach.
It is March and that means wind
and a smudged, slate sky. The bride
wears green. She shimmers. Her babies
toe the sand. They don't wear shoes.
It is almost cold. The Officiate
gathers us in a circle. A circle means
things. Charley reads Neruda in his
red shirt. She reads Rilke. *Letters*
to a Young Poet. She is green and Charley
is red. At the end, they vow to each
other: Christ said, "I commit my
spirit unto you." They say this.
They join hands. Charley has rolled
the Neruda up like a racing program.
She takes his hand, rolled poem and all.
The circle parts for them.

UPON THE BIRTH OF MIKE'S DAUGHTER, SOME UNSOLICITED ADVICE REGARDING LOVE AND OTHER SUCH VAGARIES

1. The Underworld.

I will tell you this, dear little girl,
there is a Hades and it can be found
everywhere. I imagine your course:
there will be places you go. Just as
important, there will be places you
never go. To wit: Apalachicola,
Florida. Its own kind of Underworld.
I shudder at the memory—a pea-soupy
night in March after eating succulent
oysters from a bed gone bad. Teens
in pick-ups tear down the quiet streets,
whine through their gears. If you do
not end up there on what, God willing,
will be your long, strange ride, know
that you are lucky, that it is a hell-hole.
Know, too, that it's just as hellish to love
and lose as it is to have never loved
at all. That night in Apalachicola, I saw
a thick-necked, tattooed man.
His back was rigid, his hair clipped
tight. I was afraid of him because
I believed he was ignorant. He retrieved
a woman, a barmaid with floppy
breasts. She, too, had tattoos. They

stumbled off to a Lincoln, their life
together. Hell is tattoos and oysters,
ignorance. Hell is unlucky geography.
Hell is knowing the rest of the story.

2. Orpheus & Eurydice.

Once there was a nymph—
Eurydice. Nymphs are beautiful, so she
was. Orpheus sang every chance he got.
Saturdays was karaoke.
Eurydice came into the bar bearing
her midriff as was the fashion then.
The bikers dropped their jaws.
Orpheus put down his beer and sang
her an Elvis song. They became lost
in their mutual charms. Together they
were young and pretty and in love.
They smelled good and they tasted
good and there was no place on their
bodies that was not smooth and good.
They spent blissful Apalachicola days.
It was hell.

3. An Interlude.

What I am trying to say is that hell
is. Much fruitless effort can be spent
looking for places where it is not.
But it is. Everywhere. Do you know
that I am smiling? I am smiling.

There are certain things you do not yet
know. That is probably best, but I will
tell you a secret because I can, because
soon enough you will figure it out
for yourself:

4. The Rest of the Story.

Orpheus and Eurydice had many trials.
They churned through life on the Panhandle.
They loved and lost. It ended. Orpheus sang
a sad song. And then, alone, he gave in.
His music was full. Perfect. Ripe.
It was midnight on a Saturday. No one
in the bar but him. Eurydice long gone.
Stolen by a mean old snake from Wisconsin.
There was the ubiquitous pea soup.
His throat warbled to nobody. Then he
realized the secret in a flash: Wisconsin
is just a bus ride away. Surely it is an iced-
over hell, a nightmare worse than this.
But it can be got to from here, and there
I will find my beautiful nymph.
I will be with her in the ice so our lips
freeze together. Or we will flee that old
man. We will scamper through the hellish
landscape. We will melt and we will freeze.
We will be wet, dry, thirsty, full as ticks,
rubbed raw in the genitals from love.
We will read too much and not enough.
We will snort Ritalin, shoot up. We will
abstain. We will know the word of God.
We will do things our mothers cannot

imagine. There will be unnamable
objects, acts, purity, peace. All of it is hell,
yes, but I will be singing and she will be
Eurydice and we will know everything
there is to know. Where is Wisconsin?
What if I don't remember her face?

Then he strikes out into the misty night,
blissful for the first time in days.

2.
HIGHLAND AVENUE

THE WORLD PEACE POEM

Birmingham, Alabama, May 2003

This is a day that seeks no documentation,
per se: a nothing day—later I will shampoo
the rug. There are men working on the A/C
in my apartment; it is warm. I have found
a café, an open table outside, and Highland
Avenue buzzes with a strange parade: Doo
Dah Day—people of various stripes bring
their dogs to the tidy little park down
the way. The dogs are leashed humanely—
harnesses of ingenious design. Hundreds
of smiling canine eyes, wagging tails, tongues.
Their people wear sunglasses. It's a zoo.
But a pleasant one. Tops are down. Friendly,
liberal, folksy music spills into the street.
All manner of preferences prevail. In
a place such as this, anything is possible:
a Big Blue Marble of peace, balanced budgets
everywhere, an appreciation for the world's
sundry beauties—physical, political, muscled
or not, a sprawling range of sticker prices.
There, a dachshund—taffy-stretched; here,
a Jack Russell. Yonder, a perfect mutt puppy.
Here comes a beautiful old woman in a pink dress.
There goes a Volvo, a stroller pushed happily
by a thin man and his plump wife. Now
reggae—Marley—No worry, about no thing:
Sweet songs, melodies pure and true.
Rottweilers, a Ridgeback. Dobermans in

tricked out pick-ups. Handsome, bronzed
gay men. There are silly hats, Newfoundlands.
Yappy Pekinese. Bonnie Raitt. In such a
world as this, isn't it a perennial Saturday?
Isn't it just warm enough for the Sheepdogs
to open their mouths in a smiley half-pant?
Isn't there just enough breeze? Aren't there
wispy clouds enough, blue-sky enough, poems
enough, and pretty-people-to-marry enough?
Can this very day metastasize, spread out
concentrically from our Magic City's ground
zero? When will it reach Iceland? What on earth
will they do with all that warm breeze?

THE SURFACE OF THINGS

There's a way-too-thin man-boy
And a syrup-voiced Australian.

There are some others, here,
There. The boy orders a Coke.

He walks to the TV, stands
Inches from the flatscreen.

The Aussie talks sports
With the woman who talks

Anything. *The woman-golfer*
Didn't make the cut, not this time.

The boy hops down the steps.
Something's wrong with him.

Remember the commercial
With McEnroe on top of a sky-

Scraper, he says. *I didn't really*
Like him. He was a firebrand.

The blonde outside wears
Her hair mussed just-so.

Man-boy knocks a chair. *He*
Hit that ball through a window

All the way across the way
On just the third try. *Amazing,*

She says. Man-boy's parents
Collect him. The blonde sheds

Her jean-jacket to reveal
A shimmering, pink halter.

WHY I LOVE A CITY

1.

Questions abound inside the café today:
Do mosquitoes understand this unseasonable
cold? The Hawaiian man who stands outside
in the wet, wearing Birkenstocks and Malcolm
X glasses—why did he choose to tie a balloon
there? Are those two men brothers or lovers:
and, more important, how are we to take
their shared facial structure? Skin tone?
Posture? Icy glare? Who is "Jennifer Daniels"
and why does she have her own eponymous
website? The brownish flier says she "flirts
with rock, pop and anything else that comes
into her musical path." What does that mean,
and will she flirt with me? Why am I so happy?
I am giddy. I am butterflies, honeysuckle.
Bring on the unseasonable cold, the glares,
the room-temperature mosquitoes twiddling
their thumbs.

Why do I love such a city
as this? Do mosquitoes have thumbs? They
should. Where is Carl Sandburg when you
need him? Who are my hog butchers?

Or do I write my poems at lunch—do I be-bop?

2.

A woman brings her ankle to her palm
and slaps. I am a fan of this. I am a fan
of the wonderful little girl who will not
put on her shoes in this unseasonable cold.
Her mother is the ankle-slapper. The girl
wears the #7 on her shirt; now she wears
her sandals. She be-bops down the steps.
The mother says her daughter's name,
but I cannot hear it. The girl shares her
mother's lovely dark complexion. Perhaps
her mother is Polynesian—goodness, maybe
they are tethered to the balloon man standing
outside, smoking idly by a tree!—"Take
them slowly!" says the mother. "This is not
a soft playground." Where are the soft
playgrounds? All the playgrounds I know
are blessedly hard and dirty places. Is it
there that we first learned to flirt with rock,
pop, and whatever else that comes into our
musical path?

Our paths are music.

3.

A middle-aged woman—salt-and-pepper,
Roman-nosed—comes into #7's path. She
sketches women in long, sheer dresses—
women who are nowhere to be seen. They

exist only in her dreams or in the smoky
labyrinths of her memory.

It's OK, she says.
It's OK if we talk because your mother's here.
But it's usually not a good idea to talk to strangers.

#7 giggles. They converse. In earnest. Why
has #7 chosen this woman—what pain,
what hurt, what deep, dark secret does She
of the Roman Nose think she's hiding from
the world? Does she not know that caramel-
colored cherubim roam the earth looking
through all the most likely places—coffee shops,
libraries, gray cubicles—in search of such
untouched folk?

4.

They talk:

I'm not a YMCA kind of person.

Do you have a dad?

Do I have a dad?

No, I mean a husband?

No.

Do you have a dad?

No, not anymore.

Do you like guns?

No, no, I don't like guns at all.
I don't like blood and I don't like guns.
I don't like people who hit.

I do. I like to kill people.

No you don't

I do.

5.

Yes, I am a fan of this exchange. They can
talk this way forever. They *do* talk this way
forever. #7 shares a secret: *Dentists wear*
gloves. She has a story to go with it:

A tooth
came out but her mother didn't know. Her
mother was asleep. She didn't *hear* the tooth
come out because she was asleep. So #7
took the tooth up in her tiny hand and climbed
onto her sleeping mother. *Here is my tooth.*
There was her tooth. The dentist—who wore
gloves: that's how come she knows—put
the tooth back in. The Roman-nosed woman
is amazed at this necromancy. She should be.

This is, I think, what has become of angels:

CHERUB:	*What's your favorite color?*
WOMAN:	Blue.
CHERUB:	*What's your favorite sport?*
WOMAN:	Gosh, I don't know if I have one anymore.
CHERUB:	Swimming.
WOMAN:	I used to swim two hours a day. In the ocean.
CHERUB:	*What's your favorite animal?*
WOMAN:	Dolphin or elephant.
CHERUB:	*Which one? You have to pick.*
WOMAN:	I don't know. I can't pick.

This is, I'm sure of it, the future of angels.

6.

On the door, there is another sign: *Lost: Dog—Black & Tan. 35 lbs. $500*

Just under $14.29 per pound of lost dog. What price an hour lost to a precocious little brown girl? What price lost angels, lost children, lost drawings in journals, lost sandals, lost mothers, lost oceans, lost youths, lost dads and favorite sports and teeth?

Why am I so happy? I am giddy. Butterflies
and honeysuckle. Outside a red balloon
be-bops back and forth against a telephone
pole. Somewhere a dog is lost. Bring on
this city. Bring me the city. Bring me the city
and I will drown it in love.

MUSE: THE SENATOR'S WIFE

1.

Sag Aloo Palak: creamed spinach with potatoes
and onions. A rose by any other name. This
restaurant is mirrored so it can seem larger
than it is. The water comes in metal cups
to keep it cool. Pretty Punjabi women wear
saris and float between the tables—*Everything*
is fine? Everything is fine. At the tiny bar—
that is metal too—two happy men, gay *and*
happy—sip vodka tonics, wait for an order
to-go. At a table in the back sits a lovely
woman in her sixties, a brilliant white shock
of hair. She is with a man. I can't hear either
of them—the tablas make a conspicuous
arrhythmia that gives the place a peripatetic,
insistent heartbeat that cannot be ignored.
I see her mouth, *That's so cool*. Of course.
Where else would the Sixties' unshorn Gaias
go—those easy riders, easy undulators, so easy
with their grandiose and impossible notions
of Peace? Yes, where else *could* they be? A hall
of mirrors, this oasis of Otherness, where food
is called by Other, more poetic names.

2.

Still another poetics sits in the corner: A family
tableau. There is the man—the father—who looks

just like a well-preserved senator. Handsome, grave—
no, not grave, that's not quite fair. He is serious
but he laughs. Or at least he knows when it is time
to laugh. And when he does, it's made-for-television.
Toothy, pleasant, rhythmic. His two sons are there,
as well, flanking him to either side. They are young
for him. They stare into the mirrors, make amazing
monstrous faces. They wince at the pungent little
pots of food when they arrive.

Then there's mom.
A version of Caroline Kennedy, but considerably
more beautiful. Dark and thin. She is not young
or old, per se. The boys, all three of them, are hers.
I'll say her eyes are gray; I can't quite see that far.
I'll guess they're eyes that do not soak your image
in—they shine it back at you. The boys, the younger
ones, grapple for her attention. One of them stirs
his food into a mud. She scolds him and he smiles.
The other bangs his metal cup with a spoon—a tiny
toastmaster. She puts her hand on his—he's soothed.
What, you ask, of "Senator Joe" (I've named him)?
How does he arrange himself in orbit to her sun?
His head is on a swivel. It's as if she isn't there.
He sits across from "Caroline," a woman he clearly
needs, a woman he has to have, or else he's not who
he thinks he is. And so he can't bear to look at her,
for fear she'll disappear. No—there's a question
mark after *disappear*: "...[F]or fear she'll disappear?"
Is that why he looks at everything else? Or is he
dazzled by all the scrim? Does he know the hostess
wears a weightless wrap across her throat to hide

the pink remnants of a tracheotomy? Or is it this:
At home he gets his fill—when Caroline sleeps
or bathes or puts the kids to bed, he's there,
his eye trained on every inch of her, locked in.
I don't know what it is. I'm not a senator of anything.

3.

Ah, Caroline. You don't seem to mind us star-struck
little boys at all and I'm so happy for that—for you,
for us. And this: your boy, the toastmaster, has taken
your sweet touch as an invitation. Smiling all the time,
he tugs at your slender arms then rests his hands
upon your shoulders. You stare and smile into him.
He brings his hands up to your face as if he's blind—
or maybe he's something like a sculptor. Maybe he
wants this other way to store the memory of your face:
within his fingers. You let them linger in your shiny
black hair, you move your head to and fro (How on
earth can Senator Joe not even notice *this?*) so he can
work your whole mane into a tangled, gorgeous
mess. Your lips are parted, you look dizzy, hair spills
over your face. You and your boy are as in love as you
will ever be. With anyone. Does he know that all future
loves will be measured against this very moment,
that any other beauty must somehow be as beautiful
as this? When will he decide that even close enough—
an echo somewhere, a sideways glance in a restaurant
looking glass—will somehow, someway have to do?

HISTORY LESSON: WHY ART WILL NOT SAVE THE WORLD

Real names be proof.
—D. Boon

1.

Ringo says Shea Stadium, in '65, was an asylum.
John went mad, he says. Banging the keyboard
with his *elbows*. Everyone was mad. Even
the thick-necked cops. There were buttons,
almost identical: I LOVE JOHN; I LOVE RINGO.
Girls squeezing their pretty heads in their hands,
working up to giant, manic bursts of aspiration:

PAUL!!!!!!!!!!!!!!!!!!!!!!!!!!!

GEORGE!!!!!!!!!!!!!!!!!!

Paul can't hear you, honey.
Neither can George. They'll never know. You're just
rain into their ocean.

2.

But here's the kicker: Ringo couldn't even hear
his rap-tap-tap. They all played like shit. It was just

a big excuse for 66,000 people to bubble over, dash
one by one, between a gauntlet of New York City's
Finest and a series of strategically placed barricades.
So, then, the middle-aged Colombian guy who sets
up his guitar at the coffee shop this morning, he
must know exactly what I'm talking about. He sings
things nobody's ever heard—obscure Spanish folk
songs. *In Spanish.* The long line of Unitarians frets
over the merits of lemon-poppy seed versus those
of biscotti. Only one woman listens to the songs,
and she spends her time between numbers trying
to alleviate all that ills Colombia:

Don't you think—
I've heard Colombia is very beautiful—don't you think
if Colombians could understand what they have,
they could oust the drug lords and end the civil war?
They could have eco-tourism instead. Lots of rich
people could come and spend their money and then
the Colombian people wouldn't stand for the violence
because they'd know tourists don't want to come
to a dangerous place...

She says this as he tunes his
guitar. He smiles, tells her he doesn't understand
the language very well. She starts in with her pidgin
Spanish. He has a set to play. *Ah,* finally he says,
peace very hard. No. Never peace. He smiles again,
a thank you, then he strums the neck with vigor,
launches full-bore into "The Girl from Ipanema"
and the whole world seems to prick its ears.

THE AFTERLIVES OF SMALLISH THINGS

The old woman with white
        paper cups of cat food—
She scatters sustenance. They're seeds,
        Stuff-of-Life, this bone
Mealy, crude-protein Meow Mix.

Yes, she does indeed hobble
        Herself up the steep steps
And down again, rail clutched
        In her thin avian claw
Of a hand. She disseminates

Along the way, a sower.
        She is a Johnny Appleseed.
How integral her free range
        Cattery. Nestled in among junkies
And their slow skeletal ambulations;

Just blocks from the Police
        Station, Temple Emmanuel, a curry
House, a wide open park.
        My cat-food woman may
Or may not be aware

Of religionists who wear respirators
        Just so they don't suck
Down a gnat or some
        Other tiny living, breathing thing.
Does she know they aspire

To never move, lest they
        Crush or otherwise compress something
Sentient? I don't really know.
        I do know my mother
Not long ago sat upon

Her little yellow bird, Marcel.
        She screamed and cried until
He hopped up and booked
        It around the couch, none
The worse for wear. So

It seems anyway. The vet
        Prescribed steroids to combat swelling
Of the brain—and why
        Not? You who resurrected yourself
From blackest night, consciousness wiped

Clean between my mom's rock
And the couch's hard place!
I'd have a big head
Too, Marcel. How to follow
It, now that's the trick.

Even worse, how does one
In your position live down
The fact that life's damned
Dangerous, that sentience can fly
Away, never even say goodbye?

The religionists rely on faith.
Good for them. Me too.
I have faith in resurrections.
Yours and those of others.
I believe in the dutiful

Old women who spend all
Day long remembering the forgotten
Feral cats, tossing kibble on
The stairs to the larger
City just out of view.

3.
HISTORY LESSON—PART II

THANKSGIVING

I.

In the prominently displayed photograph on the dining room wall
the junior
senator from Illinois threads
his long fingers to form
a nest for his knobby knee.

This stillness circa 2006. Year of our Lord.
Done at the City
of Washington. In these United

States.

My iPod is in the Ferrari
is what someone else has
said. Out loud.
In the present day.

It must be true

because someone said it
and I heard it.

Feng shui is a term regarding the placement of things in
relationship to other things.
　　　Things placed just so and so on:

Annie Leibovitz at Work
　　　on one of many well-placed so-called coffee tables.

This is the well-apportioned home
　　　of the prominent Lebanese-American
　　　anesthesiologist.

The fourth Thursday in November. Two thousand
　　　and twelve.
　　　McLean, Virginia.
　　　Etc.

Down the road: the Central Intelligence
　　　Agency. All manner
　　　of old money scattered
　　　along the Chain Bridge Road.

Down the road from that: the Potomac winds toward
　　　The City of Washington.

Somewhere else the cedars of Lebanon sway.
　　　Far away but not forgotten.

I'm running a taxi
says one guest. Persian. Handsome.

He's gonna run me home
says another.

She is the blonde-haired-blue-eyed White-bread American wife of another man,
the preeminent if laconic Lebanese-American
plastic surgeon who dyes
his thinning hair.
(Does he dare to eat a peach. And so on.)

I am writing in purple ink.
A too-fat line
ten feet from the kitchen.
My belly full of kibbeh nayyeh:
raw ground beef, mint leaves, onion,
olive oil,
and also falafel so perfect
no perfect-enough words exist.

Two long rooms away is Bungee
the dog.
Who sits and jumps when you ask him to.
Who eats sausages when you ask him to.
Who is himself hypo-allergenic.
Such an accommodating entity.

All night long there has been heady talk of work
at the World Bank. This, a very measurable
brand of accomplishment
anyone can understand.

Somewhere in some other room circulates a beautiful woman
far too young for me.
My brother-in-law's cousin's
daughter.

Second-generation American-
Lebanese. Brilliant.
Bespectacled. It is she who aspires
to the World Bank.
And of course her parents who aspire for her.

I am alone, unhindered, in a room impeccably wallpapered.

There's still dessert.

Mom when was the dog last out?

Now I am writing on the back of an envelope and the purple ink bleeds through
and it will be unintelligible
which is nothing new.

Two rooms away from six years ago
the handsome young senator
bores a hole through me still.

There is a habit of mind that pervades
the present age.

This is the particular stimulus.
And it leads to this.
Which leads to this.
Which leads to this.
Which is to say: Etc.
So on.

Six degrees of separation
creates a yawning
chasm.

Now I am only writing to anyone
who has the foggiest idea who
Frank O'Hara is. Ken Koch.
The NY School.

The Cedar Bar.

Pollock. Krasnick.

Kevin Bacon. Kyra Sedgwick.

Etc and so on.

Now I am only writing to anyone
who knows Hezbollah. Hamas. Who knows
the single-minded aspiration
of the University of Virginia. Georgetown.
The CIA.

I feel like you got to know the people
on campus all of us saw
but didn't know on a whole other level.

Someone says this at the party
and means it. Because I suppose
to them it's a party and
it's true.

My iPod is in the Ferrari is what the host
has said—of course he's the anesthesiologist.
The expert at knocking people out.
He is a nice man. An able host.
And he means it. It's all true
and a party to him.

The long slim finger of Lebanon:

a single road

from north to south. A country of fully
four million. A worldwide diaspora
five times that.
Seven times Beirut
is buried by the sea.
Eight times rebuilt.
Give or take.
The Paris of the Middle East.

Once

Phoenician merchants sailed everywhere the ocean went
to sell their purple dyes to heads of state.
And they shared their simpler alphabet—
twenty-two phonetic letters
making writers of everyone they ever met.

I won't say I've got the numbers right.

Counting's not my thing.

I'm only after essences.

The essence here is aspiration, attainment.
How, now, they show themselves.

There is an American tale of aspiration, attainment.
How they show themselves.
It involves various jumbled versions of the junior senator.
His unlikely path
to annunciation. Addison's disease. Shoddy papers.
A bad back. A black man for a deadbeat dad.
A war-dead better older brother.
Cabrini-Green.
Etc and so on.

There is an American tale for how the photo got to be there
on the wall in the first place.
A silent auction.
No.
Not silent.
A bidding war. Glares and arrhythmias.
I can't remember.
It aided the school. It is not interesting.

What is interesting is the photo itself.

What is interesting is its very prominent display.

The messy mixture of metaphors. Avatars.

The iPod, the Ferrari, the garage.

Etc. So on.

James or John or Charles the anesthesiologist's friend
reports that the gender neutral pronoun is now
their. This he gleaned from a tense email
one day at work. *I said,*
'Thank you! I did not know that rule had changed!'
In earnest he categorized the colleague

Who disabused him as *metrosexual*. Which is he says how
they knew.

Words are a sour perfection I'm afraid.

The mouth the tongue and lips make them.

The mouth the tongue and lips slip.

Order is important.

Now I am writing to the speech pathologists.

In the book I am now not reading there is a boy
who stammers. He is of course a poet.
A familiar shame burnt from my neck, but I nodded.
Only in my poems, I realized, do I get to say exactly *what I want.*

He says this. I swear.

He is imaginary. He is thirteen. His words, such novel things.

But still.

I am afraid I will never finish this poem.

I am afraid all the things it is about mean it is not about anything at all.

The truth is I am only writing this poem because
    I want to remember the way someone in particular
    was—is—very beautiful and when I was younger
    it seemed as if the truest way to do this was

To have your tongue in the beautiful person's
    mouth and then—at intervals—to simply softly
    slowly put your lips only your lips on her lips
    and though you weren't supposed to to open
    your eyes and wait for her to intuit you and open
    hers too at which point you kiss her nose her chin
    and her forehead her neck her ears and then her
    lips again of course and again and again and again—

Somewhere in all this you imagine she must shut her eyes
    again
    so that you can kiss them
    —her eyes—
    indiscriminately too.

Now truth and memory are mute when it comes
to the awkward clacking of our heavy-
framed spectacles.

Now truth and memory say nothing of the new gusts
outside announcing the cold front and how too
soon I will run with my brother-in-law and his wife
my sister to his big black German car. Far away from
anyone's soft warm breath perfectly
sour with Malbec.

There is the kind of aspiration or dream
that leads us to be photographed by Annie Leibovitz.

———————————— that leads us to anesthesiology.
—————————————————— a common
language.
—————————————————— Ferraris.
—————————————————— the World
Bank.
—————————————————— the New World.
—————————————————— Mars and Harvard
Business School.

Now I pine away and imagine things.
My Malbec kiss. Etc and so on.

Now a new photo of Dickinson has surfaced.
The face is young. Gender-neutral.
Growling. From somewhere inside.
A real human body is attached to me—
say the eyes.

She tied together for us with string the unattached pieces
of what she'd written and boxed it all up.
What she was imposing upon us, posterity.
The inscrutable running transcript.

The habit of her mind.

There is no longer an Elizabeth
Bishop in the world.
What's left now is just fish and armadillos.
Disembodied antic moans at the dentist's.
This regards essential identities. The I. The Other.
Etc. So on.
Each night the sky in this world explodes.

II.

The poet is the curator of beauty.

Now he finds himself in the Baltimore-Washington International
airport scribbling on a thigh-
high counter in a bar—still another
indiscriminately beautiful
woman at half-an-arm's
length, pecking at her impeccable
Cupertino machine.

In eight hundred crow-flown miles
he'll be home.
He'll have the house all to himself.
(Does he dare to eat a peach. Blah blah and so on.)

Now again Burberry is a thing.

Pork-pie hats. Berets.

The portly bartender pulls him a Magic Hat.
The glass itself an hourglass.

Then the tipsy co-ed at the bar. Beautiful
Too in her way.
She wrestles with her
Overcoat as the handsome young man

In his *Ithaca* hoodie sips his Jack and Coke
and makes his impossible play.
Where are you headed?
What's your name?
Blah blah e-t-c and so on.

Shorthand to say what can't be
said.

The ways she is beautiful:
elegant unobtrusive bones of her wrist. Each breast
a pert, pristine handful.
Nose that would be rendered on paper
in two dimensions with just a suggestion
of two quick afterthought jots.

Too soon
she staggers off into the bright blue fluorescence.
The young man just grins
this 3-D loss away.

I spy him later on the seamless conveyor belt.
Alone save for the elegant gadget
pressed hard against his ear.
He stands stock-still and is conveyed.
Mired in conversation with his
mother I'm afraid. It seems she
won't shut the fuck up.

I am afraid this is a world where we will always have someone
or something else
in our ear.

I am afraid this is a world wherein the men
line up at the filthy airport urinals
and one young man won't take the open
trough because he's afraid another man
to either side of him will get a fleeting glance
at what may in fact be his insignificant cock.
The gesture—*Can I go ahead of you?*
He yields. "I'm good," he says it even
Out loud.
Which can't be true.
If you were good
you wouldn't even be here.

I am not imagining anymore.

Now I am making a case for all the curators
            in this mostly unmitigated Information
            Age.

So much to collect and sort:

Which is to say
Another story but the truth—

In an airport Americans talk. And drink
            and watch TV. They talk out loud
            to no one or each other.
            Whichever or both.

The Sunday after Thanksgiving.

This is the busiest American travel day of the year.

Things a poet hears in this ubiquitous new age Purgatory:

> *Daddy can you walk smaller?*
> *I love you so much I miss you terribly Mary.*
> *I'm a 49er fan. Joe Montana. Jerry Rice.*
> *Let it go! Let it go!*

That was poetry in motion baby.
O man! Jesus. Dream come true. O my god no.
I like the way you think.
I try to avoid O'Hare at all costs.
I don't think they ever knew it would grow to that extent.
The only airport I was ever forced to sleep in was in O'Hare. It was two hours in the hotel then come right back no sense in leaving.
I love my city though. I love my city.
No flags. That's a beautiful thing. Just desserts.
And right before halftime. Eleven seconds.
I can't read that far.
Not that many seconds left.
That's the great thing about America. You got that time to dick around. My dad's from India. You're in there. You're not in there, you're on a work farm.

Did I say there is a new kind of quarterback?
There is a new kind of quarterback.

Reads. Runs. Throws of course. Thinks.
He's inked up.
Impossible to understand
this new world order for those of us born
of the White-bread 20th Century.

But the story:

The man next to me—we're still at the airport bar—says:
I'd like an order of the French fries and an Obrycki's lager
and I'd like those things well done. Hello hi mom—hello?
Yes. What's up? Hold on. Hi dad hold on. Hello mom?
. . . And the rest of the family and everyone's shit and Bram's and Wayne's.

The terrible football game on the flatscreen.

One woman reads Stieg Larsson or his reasonable
    facsimile at the adjacent two-top.

The man next to me is in IT. He announces it
    to her.
    He joins her so confidently.
    She accepts him so openly.
    They banter so cheerfully
    against the white noise background:

The coolest thing about Key West is Ernest Hemingway's roosters.
Are you kidding?
I'm in IT.
You got all the gadgets.
I just turned 26.
English! Totally useless!
My parents are doctors.
Jews started basketball!
Did Jews start basketball?!
Your erectile dysfunction could be a problem of blood flow.
You should know I heal very quickly.
Last Christmas that was a huge gash.
Don't ever undermine my intelligence and make me feel inferior to you.

Needless to say words bleed into other words. I hear everything
    at once.

The one is exactly as attractive as the other one.
    Which is to say: sort of.
    This is a beautiful confluence.
    Rarer than love.

I am afraid I will never finish this poem.

All the things it is about mean it is not about anything at all.

We live in a world where things change for no reason:
          six-toed cats become roosters. And so on.

It is crass. Chaotic. Vulgar, drunken. Half-baked and misshapen.

But cut to the chase:

I want to know right now the chances they will fuck.
          The IT guy and the 26-year-old bibliophile.

The world can be saved if they find a way to fuck.
          Excuse my French
          but I do vote they fuck. You do too.

Now they are discussing the real-life nature of mead.
          Viscosity. Bitterness.

Earlier: Beowulf. This leads to that and so on.

He is hirsute.
          He says *faux* 4G.
          This is a real thing in the new world.

As is her singing laugh.
She leans in.

So okay, yes:

Let's let ourselves believe they someday have a chance.

III.

A sturdy, blue-blazer dad and his daughter, in the corporate coffee store. Weeks and hundreds of miles later. The man reads the newspaper. A numb and flat-faced boy has shot up his mother's elementary school then turned the gun upon himself. The little girl wears a white church dress trimmed in pink. Her glittery hair accessory perched like a tiara atop her head. "But he's crazy," she tells her father. This is why it isn't dangerous. This is why it isn't real. It is Sunday. A comfy leather couch in the loft space up above the whir and screech below. Three gray-headed men: one handsome in a cable-knit sweater reading a slim, heady volume; the other two ugly, non-descript. One watches a shoot-em-up movie on his laptop, buds plugged deep into his hairy ears. He should be furtive but he's not. The other stares into what passes in this place for space. Plastic domes adorn the iced coffee drinks.

I'm afraid we're doomed.

An insistent day-long rain promises itself to us. Early winter soak and sog.

Ready Freddie? says the man again. He folds the paper with all its words and ads, its murderers, and then he tucks it underneath his arm. The girl reaches up and takes this father's free hand in hers.

Fearless, steady. The both of them.

This way, together,
they descend again into the world.

ACKNOWLEDGMENTS

"Upon the Thirtieth Anniversary of Hank Aaron Surpassing Babe Ruth as All-Time Homerun King" first appeared in *Birmingham Weekly.*

"Upon Charley's Marriage to a Girl from Idaho" and "Upon the Birth of Mike's Daughter, Some Unsolicited Advice Regarding Love and Other Such Vagaries" first appeared in *Harpur Palate.*

"The World Peace Poem" was anthologized in *Whatever Remembers Us: An Anthology of Alabama Poetry*, edited by Sue Brannan Walker (Negative Capability Press, 2007).

"Why I Love a City" first appeared in *International Poetry Review.*

"An Aubade for the African Queen and Its Big Bang" first appeared in *Sliver of Stone.*

Many thanks to the editors, and thanks to Ben Gunsberg, Stuart Flynn, Anne-Wyman Black, Iris Rinke-Hammer, Charley Henley, and Mike Hamilton for reading and responding to earlier versions of some of these poems.

TJ Beitelman is a writer and teacher living in Birmingham, Alabama. He's published a novel, *John the Revelator*, and two collections of poetry: *In Order to Form a More Perfect Union* and *Americana*, all from Black Lawrence Press. His stories and poems have appeared widely in literary magazines, and he's received fellowships from the Alabama State Council on the Arts and the Cultural Alliance of Greater Birmingham. He taught writing and literature at Virginia Tech, where he earned an M.A. in English, and at the University of Alabama, where he earned an M.F.A. in creative writing and also edited *Alabama Heritage* and *Black Warrior Review*. Since 2002, he has taught creative writing at the Alabama School of Fine Arts in Birmingham, and he's an Artist in Residence at the Gorham's Bluff Institute on Sand Mountain in northeast Alabama. He can be found on-line at www.tjbman.com and at www.try101.org.